Mining the Past

Mining the Past

Vignettes of the Arnold-Schuster Family Tree

Charles P. Arnold, Jr., Ph.D.

Library of Congress Control Number: 2013921025
ISBN: Hardcover   978-1-4931-4560-7
                 Softcover   978-1-4931-2970-6
                 eBook   978-1-4931-2971-3

Rev. date: 11/27/2013

To order additional copies of this book, contact:
Xlibris LLC
1-888-795-4274
www.Xlibris.com
Orders@Xlibris.com
143261

Table of Contents

To our Grandchildren
And
To Their Grandchildren

Introduction

OUR FAMILY HISTORY reminds me of an aged tree which stands tall and proud even as it has weathered difficult storms throughout its history. And like the one on our cover which looks beyond itself to the great hills surrounding it, this family has for many, many generations, in the words of the Psalmist, lifted its eyes to the hills and testified from whence its strength had come—from the Lord, the maker of heaven and earth.

I am the son of Mildred (Nee Clayton) and Charles Perry Arnold, Sr., both of whom have died. I came to be what I would call a serious minded writer late in life. I had always been a prodigious writer and loved spending time writing. As a scientist I wrote and published scientific papers throughout my career. As a meteorologist with the United States Air Force I wrote numerous papers published and mostly unpublished concerning tropical cyclones using satellite data. And as theology has always been an avocation of mine I cannot say when I wasn't writing short essays on that subject. But it wasn't until 2007 that I decided to publish some of these theological subjects. After being duly humbled by that experience I have once again collected what I had found through another avocation of mine, genealogy, and having assembled it decided to publish it—the result being this book.

When that interest first began I really cannot say. I do know that when my eldest daughter Amy needed to bring her family tree to class for study, around 1974, I helped assemble as much information as I had available at the time. Though that interest has always remained and I have collected all the keepsakes and letters and recollections that I could over the years I was unable to do much with that until the advent of the desktop computer and more specifically, the advent of such wonderful programs as Ancestry.com, the database of The Church of Jesus Christ of Latter-Day Saints at Familysearch.org, and other available genealogical search engines both domestic and foreign on the internet.

What I found was a gold-mine of family nuggets. For a researcher such as I who loves to work alone and dig through tons of data and data sources it was like a child in a sandbox with many different toys. I had the same kind of experiences doing this research as I had while trying to understand the morphology of tropical cyclones in the Pacific Ocean using high resolution satellite imagery. There were many disappointments, problems, hurdles, and even shocks that had to be worked through with all but a few of those people who are mentioned in the following pages, but there were also many aha moments similar I believe to what the Greek Archimedes may have experienced during his Eureka bath experience. One grandmother left home at the age of 17 for a vacation in Florida and returned with a husband; a grandfather and a great grandmother were discovered to have been born out of wedlock; another grandfather committed suicide while another grandmother and her sisters were put into an orphans home so her father might bring more boys into the world to help support his family. And then there were the pleasant discoveries of villages in Germany with such quaint names as Hohenfelde, Warmersdorf, Schonbrunn and Parkentin where church records told of family member baptisms, confirmations, and marriages. On the branches of our combined family tree we find a teacher, musicians, joiners and cabinet makers, farmers, firemen, a glazier, military veterans, and individuals with strong Christian faiths.

I delved into Federal and Foreign Census records, marriage records, death certificates, city directories, newspaper clippings, cemetery grave stone photos, city maps, personal trips and conversations with family members, etc. I found some Census records were plum full of information. The 1900 U.S. Federal Census, for example, includes such information as month and year of birth for each named member of a family, the number of years the husband and wife had been married, the total number of children the mother had given birth to and the number of those still living, the place of birth of each individual, education levels for each member, as well as the place of birth of their mothers and fathers. Also included was the year of immigration and whether the individual had been naturalized or not and the type of employment for each member of the family. City Directories provided addresses for home and work and the type of work the individual was engaged in at the time. Since businesses were also included in these directories I found they were very helpful. The enumeration dates were found to be important if it were required to know the person's age I was looking for was before or after the census had been taken. Others such as the earliest 1810 to 1840 Census records were far less informative, giving only names of head of household members, and a broad age group to which each belonged—somewhat helpful but often disappointing and requiring substantial amounts of cross-checking and verifying.

From this collection of data and from family photos, letters and postcards, birth certificates, marriage and divorce documents, etc., I was able to complete my family tree for three of the four sets of my great grandparents, for four of the eight sets of my second great grandparents, and for four of the sixteen sets of my third great grandparents. But to use the word "complete" is an overstatement. As the reader will find, in a few instances there was considerable detail for the couples, while for others there was very little information about the couple. What I hope to have accomplished is to have answered the questions who, what, where, and when as best I could from all I had to work with.

Each member of two sets of my great grandparents had been born in Germany while each member of the other two sets had been born in England. Both spouses of three of the four sets had emigrated. Both members of a fourth set were born in England but it was only their son, my paternal grandfather who emigrated. Finally, both members of one set which had originally come from Germany were found to have been very early pioneers who had moved from Maryland to Virginia to Pennsylvania and then westward into Ohio. This family's German roots go back to the 18th century.

For my wife, the family tree was somewhat easier. Three of her grandparents were born in Germany and had immigrated to America while one had come from parents born in Hungary. I have found her great grandparents for two of those grandparents born in Germany as well as her great grandparents born in Hungary.

For each individual in our combined family tree I generated a document, which provides a list of all personal items and genealogical data collected for that person. Personal items include photos of the individual, letters and postcards they wrote or received, birth, baptismal and confirmation certificates, marriage records and certificates, death certificates and obituary notices, gravesite photos, newspaper clippings, etc. Genealogical data includes all those mentioned above. These data were then organized into individual manila folders, and stored in cardboard boxes.

It was from these data that a few couples and individuals were selected to have short vignettes written of them. I hope this work may encourage the reader to pursue his or her own genealogical research efforts. At least the reader may want to do as I have done. Ask someone in the family to be the steward of your treasured family genealogy after you have passed on. They needn't do anything with the material except keep it safe and secure to be one day turned over to a member of the younger generation of the family with the same instructions—unless of course they would like to use the source data to write a new story or book, or do further genealogical research themselves adding to the collection. Hopefully at some point in the future, one will be so inclined to write a good story and publish it about your family. I started the process for my family but fully expect it to continue in the future. America is now a nation that has been in existence for a long enough time for its citizens to begin to treasure their past. We must therefore make every effort to do so.

The reader may also find one of the family names in our family tree to be the same as one in his or her own tree. Hopefully if this were to be the case, what I have discovered may prove to be helpful in your research. I was able to have benefited in this manner while working on one branch of my tree. Among the family branches mentioned in this small book are Clayton, Arnold, Karnuth, Garlow, Heines, Cuppett, Spahr, Gastmeier, Roth, Wilk, Schuster, Vogtmann, Joestlein, and Weckesser. While these names may seem to be quite a few, one must remember that with each parent we have 2 grandparents, 4 great grandparents, 8 second great grandparents, and 16 third great grandparents for a total of 62 people who preceded each of us. So the 16 people on my side of the tree mentioned in the following pages represent only a fraction of those in these four generations. But if you add your spouse to this mix, as I have done, you will have 124 people to consider in which case the 24 or so individuals mentioned would amount to only 19% of the total. I believe the reader would agree that to fill in all those branches on any family tree would indeed be a formidable, if not impossible, task but I want to assure you that any work you do in this direction would be immensely rewarding and certainly worth the effort. And so I want to encourage the reader to begin this work if they have not already done so. It is worthwhile to just know one's grandparents and so—

The first couple I want to introduce you to will be Anna and John Clayton. These were the author's maternal grandparents. I lived with Anna until I was married and left home for the Air Force with a new wife. Anna was without a doubt the most influential and important person in those early years. I can honestly say that without her being so persistent and patient with me during my years as an undergraduate struggling with German, I would never have completed all the requirements later on for my doctorate. From her I learned the value of persistence. She always seemed so quiet and unassuming, but her life was anything but unassuming as we shall see. She often suffered but she was strong and resolute and always colorful. I loved her dearly.

The second couple, Rose and John Roth, is the story of my wife's maternal grandparents. This is the story of a girl who was given up, along with her two sisters, to a Lutheran run orphanage so that in her words, her handicapped father could hopefully bring more boys into the world. In spite of her many difficulties in life she practiced the presence of God in the manner of Brother Lawrence and in so doing influenced my life and Elaine's as well as that of many others whom she knew.

Fay and Fred Arnold were my paternal grandparents. Fred an Englishman photographer from the big city of London meets Fay, a farm girl from the small mid-west town of Findlay Ohio. This is the story of where and how they met, fell in love, and began to raise a family, first in Florida and later returning to Ohio. Fred struggled to become a photographer through the depression years but often had to settle for odd jobs to keep his family together.

George and Barbara Schuster were Elaine's paternal grandparents. Both emigrated from nearby villages in Bavaria, Germany, but only found each other in Pittsburgh, Pennsylvania. One arrived at Ellis Island, a young adult, while the other arrived at the port in Baltimore fourteen years earlier as a twelve year old. Through the church, they meet, marry, and settle in Pittsburgh. George, the son of an unmarried girl, became a master craftsman carpenter while Barbara was a devoted and loving homemaker and grandmother.

We will then look at the life of two of my four great grandparent couples, Perry and Margaret Garlow, a pioneering couple from Ohio and Pennsylvania whose grandparents had been German immigrants, and Frederick and Wilhelmina, German immigrants and the parents of Anna Clayton from our first story. In this vignette we find that Wilhelmina too was like George in the previous story, the result of an unwanted pregnancy but who was able to renew her life in America.

A short sidebar at this point will look at the life of Fay Arnold's brother Jacob Garlow, who left his small farm town in western Ohio and moved to Bakersfield, California. There Jacob became a very successful oilman. In the years that followed he became rich and traveled widely.

Our final two stories concern two of my second great grandparent couples. The first, Peter and Catherine Garlow, tells the story of Perry Garlow's parents, a young couple that raised a family of 11 children on the western edge of early 19th century America. This was a time when roaming bands of Shawnees still visited chaos upon the early settlers of western Maryland. The second, Maria and the Day Laborer tell of a family secret kept, or the truth of which had been lost, until it was revealed in an obscure German document I had in my possession and finally translated by a German genealogist from Rostock Germany.

Genealogy is in many ways very limited when it comes to learning about our ancestors. Living with people is really the only way to know them, their passions, their limitations, their politics, and above all, at least in my opinion of human relationships, their faith and spiritual walk in life. However, even then one may never be able to mine such nuggets from their family members as they would really like to have. I lived with and knew my step-father for over 60 years, but could never tell you what his worries were, his hopes as a young man, his dreams or what his faith really meant to him. He simply kept his thoughts under lock and key it seemed. But genealogy does result in the best we can hope to know about our past in lieu of not having had a living relationship with an individual or a fruitful relationship with those we did live with but which provided few answers freely when sought. And it is from such historical data that fictional myths and stories are made. I have tried to avoid this road, however, as I am not inclined with my scientific background to do so. As I noted earlier I will leave that to someone more talented and with much greater literary skill among my descendants. On the contrary, these stories have revealed the truths about a number of failures of those in this combined Arnold and Schuster family tree. We read of divorce, suicide, illegitimate births, and even abandonment of children. Perhaps it was shame that caused these events to become family secrets which only now are being revealed. But while these tests of faith unfolded in the lives of our family ancestors, they were met with resolute determination to press on and overcome. And it has become evident that these very strong and positive traits of character have been passed down to the current generations of Arnold-Schuster descendants.

Since it is often very confusing to figure out how one member of a family tree is related to another, I have endeavored to help the reader in this by creating a Table of relationships which I have labeled Explanation of Cousins. It may be found in the Appendix. Whoever you assign as the parent(s) from any given generation, you can then put their children, grandchildren, great grandchildren, etc. into the appropriate boxes. By picking any individual from a row and a second individual from a column where the two intersect determine their relationship to one another. The reader may also extend the Table if necessary.

I am deeply indebted to the following individuals for their assistance in researching the material for this book. First and foremost, to my wife Elaine for all her encouragement, suggestions, corrections, and memories of her family. Also to her sister Judy Agnew for the many mementos she had kept and provided me for my use in this book. Elaine's brother George Schuster provided much needed assistance with piecing together the story of his great-grandmother Wickesser. I would also like to acknowledge my cousin in California Tim Garlow who helped identify second, third, and even fourth great grandfathers on the Garlow side of our family tree. To all my cousins in Findlay Ohio, especially my dear cousin Dorthey, whose sister Mary Byal and brother Bill Garlow and their extended family hosted Elaine and I during a genealogical field trip in 2008; to my half-brothers David Arnold who provided me with many photos and mementos of our father and his parents and Edward Mains who added material about our mother Mildred and grandmother Anna Clayton; and finally, to my dear friend Ulrike Schwarz of Rostock Germany who provided immeasurable help in translating old German Script and locating, scanning, and mailing birth, baptism, and other essential documents about my second great grandmother Gastmeier who lived in Hohenfelde Germany, I will be forever grateful. To all these people and to others I have failed to acknowledge properly I herein apologize.

*"People will not look forward
to posterity who never look
backward to their ancestors"*

Edmund Burke

Charles P. Arnold, Jr., Ph.D.
Upper Marlboro, Maryland
November 2013

"Both justice and decency require that we should bestow
On our forefathers an honorable remembrance"

Thucydides

Our Grandparents

Anna Augusta Louisa Carolina Karnuth And
John William Clayton

MY MATERNAL GRANDMOTHER, was affectionately known to me as Grossmütter, German for grandmother, and less frequently Gram. But for this story she will be known primarily as others knew her, Anna. Anna was born on 25 January 1891 to German immigrant parents Ferdinand (1853-1931) and Wilhelmina (1865-1939) Karnuth and at her baptism was given the name Anna Augusta Louisa Carolina. Carolina was her Grandmother Karnuth's first name, Anna, one of her grandmother Gastmeier's middle names, and Augusta perhaps after her step-grandfather August Stier, but the source of Louisa still remains a mystery. Her parents are known to have had 6 children, five of which survived. Ferdinand Heinrick Ernst, born on 4 Oct 1887 and baptized on 6 Nov 1887 is believed to have been the only one to have died.

Anna was baptized in March 1891 by Pastor F.C. Weidmann, at her family's church of Immanuel Lutheran, a German speaking congregation in Olean, New York where she was born. The witnesses were her mother Wilhelmina, her uncle Martin Gastmeier, and August Stier, Wilhelmina's step-father.

In 1900 the Federal Census, enumerated on 15 June of that year, recorded Anna, a 9 year old living with her parents and her four siblings—Amelia, born in 1884, Henry, in 1885, Friederich in 1888, and William in 1893—at their home on 361 Buffalo Street in Olean. Her grandmother Maria, known then as Mary and married to August

Stier, lived next door with Wilhelmina's brother, Martin Gastmeier, an interesting and somewhat mysterious story in itself, which remains so to this day.

I feel privileged to have known Anna's brother Friederich, whom we all called Uncle Fritz, and her sister Amelia, whom we called Aunt Meal. Fritz was married to Aunt Evelyn who lived to be a 100 years old, many of those years spent at a Lutheran home in Canton Ohio. My wife and I often visited Aunt Evelyn at St. Luke's home during visits to Akron. She once described to us what we would today call a near death experience, of which she had never heard of before we explained it to her. After suffering a heart attack in her 90's she described herself to us as floating above her body and observing doctors who successfully revived her. And she loved her confirmation verse, Psalm 121.1 which reads *"I lift up my eyes to the hills—where does my strength come from? My help comes from the Lord, the maker of heaven and earth"*, which I paraphrased in the opening words of this book.

My fondest memories of her husband Fritz were those times as a young boy, when I was given the opportunity to be with this great-uncle and aunt for a day at their home while my parents were off doing business. There were always dishes of candy on the end tables of Evelyn's home. Hershey chocolate kisses were her favorites. Fritz loved to chew tobacco and during my visits I would sit intently watching him to see if he would miss hitting his spittoon from his chair across the room. He never missed as I recall, moving a mouth full of tobacco juice through his lips and along a graceful parabolic arc smack dab into his spittoon. And what was more surprising to me was that Aunt Evelyn never complained; at least in my hearing of what, I was later told by my mother, was a disgusting habit.

The daughter of my grandmother's sister Amelia, Gertrude Dice, was someone my grandmother loved to visit annually in Florida. Gertrude and Bill Dice had bought a new home in Punta Gorda when development was first being undertaken there on the Gulf coast. A few years ago while Elaine and I were vacationing in Punta Gorda, we visited where this home had been along one of the many canals in the city. We found only a vacant lot, the home having been destroyed by a hurricane.

But I digress. One of the popular pastimes of early 1900's family life would be reading the Bible together as a family in the evening. There was no television of course and radio itself was in its infancy. The moving picture was just being developed[1]. Bible reading was not only encouraged because it increased one's

---

[1]   Sources for life in the early decades of the 1900's include *http://www.helium.com/ items/2302645-everyday-life-in-america-in-the-early-1900s and http://kclibrary.lonestar. edu/decade00.html*

understanding of Scripture, it also taught literacy as well. And for a Lutheran family, every child is taught from Luther's Catechism and is expected to memorize sections of the catechism before becoming a member of the church. So after her two mandatory years of catechism study, Anna was confirmed in 1904 in the same church she had been baptized in, Immanuel Lutheran, and by the same Pastor, F.C. Weidmann. Besides her and another girl, there were 6 boys in the confirmation photo along with their pastor. She and the others are shown proudly holding their confirmation certificates and a small Lutheran songbook along with the New Testament and Psalter, all in German, as that was the language of the Lutheran church as it accommodated German immigrants. Besides this picture, there is also her confirmation certificate hanging prominently on a wall in my study. And the two books, gold stamped with her name and year, 1904, they are on my bookshelf of beloved old books.

By 15 June of 1908 Gram had graduated from North Olean High School. Her diploma shows that she took numerous advanced academic classes for the time. And already being fluent in German she took three years of that language together with two years of Latin along with four years of English grammar, poetry, and English literature. Following her graduation she applied for and subsequently enrolled in the State Teachers College in Buffalo New York.

This first decade of the 1900's was one of progressive education in the United States. The first elementary school was founded by John Dewey at the University of Chicago and Italian educator and physician Maria Montessori became known for her new teaching methods. However, teacher pay throughout this decade never rose much above 325 dollars. While at the State Normal and Training School, Anna lived on her own at 184 Franklin Street according to a 1910 City Directory. This would have been close to the school as she would have either walked or used the common mode of transportation of the day, the bicycle. There were after all only 8000 cars in the United States at this time with only 10 miles of paved roads. She graduated with a teaching certificate on 21 June 1910. I don't recall ever learning whether she held a teaching position during the remaining years she lived in Olean, but I do know she taught for a few years in Akron. I remember on several occasions that a former student of hers would see the two of us when we were in town together and having a fond memory of her, say hello and ask about her. I always felt that for her to leave home, live on her own, and attend college with the intent of being able to provide for herself in 1910 was the mark of a very special young woman, especially since most men worked and most women stayed at home choosing to be housewives.

Ten years earlier, in the 1900 Federal Census taken in Buffalo, New York, enumerated on 5 June of that year, John Clayton was 12 years old and living with his father, William, step-mother Catherine and 7 siblings at 238 Normal Ave. in Buffalo,

New York. John came from a blended family, for his father William, born in England had been previously married to John's mother who had also given birth to his two brothers Walter and Harry and two sisters, Anna and Jessie. Since these five children of William were born in New York and the census reports their mother had been born in England, John's mother must have lived until he, the youngest was born in 1888. In fact the answer was found when all the information available in the 1900 census was finally gleaned. We learn that William and Catherine had been married 9 years. So having been married in 1891 it can be deduced that John's mother died during his birth or very shortly thereafter since William had remarried by 1891. Furthermore all three of William and Catherine's children, May, born in 1898, Albert, born in 1895, and the oldest Paul, born in 1894, were born between 1891 and 1900.

I believe it was while Anna was attending college there in Buffalo that she met John William Clayton, her future husband. John was employed at the Electric City Glass Co. there on 480 Genesee Ave. in Buffalo, making Art Glass. The company was listed in the 1910 City Directory. One of my keepsakes is a photo of him standing with six co-workers in front of the Glass Company. There are some seven examples of the type of art glass that this company made in the two store windows behind them. In Figure 1 John Clayton stands in the middle of the picture and behind him one can see the Art Glass for sale in the store windows. In the window of my study I have a treasured piece of this art glass which he used to frame a picture of him and Anna (Fig 2). When the Sun begins to rise in the summer months, the center glass pieces at the top and bottom, shaped as roses, shimmer with beautiful hues and are the first things I see as I awake from sleep in my recliner chair next to this window each morning.

I noted from the 1910 city directory of Buffalo that John listed himself as a glazier. This prompted me to research the world of art glass in the early 20th century. Most of what follows was found in various sites on the internet and I have used such material with apologies to these sites for any errors that may be found. First, I found that art glass is defined "for the late 19th and early 20th centuries as any of the several varieties of glass using combinations of colors, special effects of opaqueness, transparency, streaking, etc., to create an aesthetic effect." Objects of art include church and synagogue windows, sun catcher window panels, as I would call them and as used in homes, such as mine. Other uses include lamps, vases, and the like.

A glazier such as John used to describe himself does glazing, which derives from the Middle English for 'glass'. Now an art glass glazier, selects, cuts, installs, replaces, and removes the glass. Lead-lights or leaded lights are decorative windows made of small sections of glass supported in lead cames. A came is a divider bar used between small pieces of glass to make a larger glazing panel, sometimes referred to as "leaded glass", this process is then referred to as "leading". The technique of creating windows using glass and lead came is called came glasswork. The term leadlight could be used to describe all windows in which the glass is supported by lead, but traditionally, a distinction is made between stained glass windows and lead-lights, the former being associated with the ornate windows of churches and other such works of architecture and the latter with the windows of commercial and domestic architecture and defined by its simplicity.

Since the traditional technique of setting glass into lead cames is the same in both cases, in the late 20th century the divisions between "leadlight" and "stained glass" became blurred, and the terms are now often used interchangeably for any window employing this technique, while the term "stained glass" is often extended to apply to any windows, sculpture, and works of art using colored glass. There is, as might well be expected, a great deal more to this art form than I have described above, but hopefully the reader will have a bit more of an appreciation of what my grandfather's work entailed and enjoy looking at the art glass of that era on the internet.

By 1913, some three years following her graduation from the Buffalo Normal School, the two decided to marry and did so on 25 June of that year. They were married at Anna's church in Olean by Pastor Weidmann. And on 20 June 1917 their first child, a daughter who one day would become my mother, Mildred Winifred Clayton, was born (Fig 3). Though no record was found that she was teaching, I believe Anna may have taught during these four years before my mother was born. A second child was born in 1921, my uncle Harold. Then a third child, Jack William was born to the couple on 20 June 1922 but trajectly died one year, 9 months, and 17 days later. Years later when Harold married he would name his first daughter Jackie in memory of this beloved brother.

The Olean city directories listed their addresses for the years that followed in 1918, 1922, 1925, 1928, and 1930. In 1918 they lived at 1880 Buffalo Street with daughter Mildred, while John was now employed as a welder of the leaded glass he made at the Olean Glass Company on 1409 Buffalo Street, within walking distance of home. My uncle told me that his father would frequently be called to a nearby catholic church to repair one of their stained glass windows vandalized by some boys. So John was able to continue the work he was doing in Buffalo when he met Anna and moved to Olean. And my mother would often tell me that when she had been scolded by her mother, that she would sit on the front doorstep waiting for her father to come home from work. She had pinched her cheeks to make it appear she had been crying and thereby obtain favor from her father. So if this particular event has any value at all perhaps it may be that John Clayton, an Englishman, had a bit more sympathy for his children than Anna, who had come from a strong disciplinarian German family.

From John's Draft Board registration on 5 June 1917, we learn that his birthday was 6 May 1888 and that he and Anna were still at 1880 Buffalo Street. During this registration it is to be noted that he requested a deferment from the draft so that he could support his young very pregnant wife. As it turned out this visit to his draft board was made just 15 days before Anna gave birth to his daughter Mildred. By 1922 the city directory had the family living at 110 S 12th Street. The 1924 directory was the only one which listed all three of the Clayton children including Jack who would die that spring on the 7th of April. In this same directory we find that John's father William John Clayton, now 68 years old was living, apparently, with only his 26 year old daughter May. It is believed that John's father may have died the following year as by then May was living in a boarding house in New York City working as a sales lady.

But by the first of June 1925 when the New York State Census was taken, we learn that John and Anna made their home at 1219 W. State Street in Olean and that Anna's parents Ferdinand, now age 71 and Minnie, 59 were living close by at 1301 W. State Street. Perhaps the thought of the loss of their son Jack prevented them from staying on at 110 S 12th Street. Ferdinand was still employed, working as a lawn grader and what we did not know previously was that he had immigrated originally to Buffalo in 1879. Living with John, now 37, and Anna 34, were their two remaining children Mildred age 7 and Harold age 4. John was still employed with the glass company. His age of 37 once again provides a year of 1888 as the year he was born which agrees with his Draft Registration date of birth. The directories from 1926 through 1930 have the family still at this same address.

John, for reasons unknown must have suffered periods of deep depression, for he unexpectedly took his life one Sunday morning on the 19th of April 1931. Uncle Harold told me only late in both of our lives that he had been the one to find his father who had hanged himself. Perhaps John was thinking of his son Jack's short life and death that same month seven years earlier. Or perhaps he was thinking of his father William who had died six years earlier. These were also difficult financial times in the wake of the great depression. There is evidence that John's work in the art glass industry had perhaps dried up and that he had turned to work as a welder for a railroad company in Olean. At this point in Anna's life and that of her two children things began to change dramatically for all of them. Figure 4 shows the gravesite of John, buried next to his son Jack. They were buried in Allegheny cemetery in Olean New York.

Anna's older sister Amelia who was by then living with her husband Ed White in Akron, Ohio at 515 Massillon Road may have asked Anna to move to Akron. It was in fact no later than 1933 that Anna had moved from Olean to live with her sister until she was able to get settled on her own. The Akron city Directory of 1933 shows that her, Mildred and Harold were living at this address and she is noted as being a widow in the directory. But very shortly she found a home less than a half a mile away on Springfield Center Road which she bought and moved her two children into.

I believe that it was in these early years in Akron that Anna also learned to drive and had bought herself a car which she would have been able to use to drive to work at a nearby elementary school where she would have taught. Mildred was graduating from East High School and her younger brother, Harold who had by now a job working as an attendant at a Sunoco gas station on Triplett Blvd, a mile or so from home as it turned out was the youngest graduate ever from East High School at the age of 15. One of his proudest achievements was his having been elected into the National Honor Society. He cherished this medal.

I can actually recall visits to Anna's home when I could not have yet been 5 years old. Harold was often found sitting around his mother's kitchen table with a few friends having a beer and without my mother's nor his mother's notice, would offer me a sip from his bottle. Also just fifty yards or so in the direction of Massillon Road on the corner with Springfield Center Road there was a small gas station with one of those old metal Pepsi coolers filled with ice and delicious "pop" including my favorite, Pepsi cola. Being offered one of these became a lasting memory of mine as well as on occasion being able to pick out candy sticks from large glass jars behind the counter of a drug store directly across Massillon Road from Gram's house. Figure 5 was taken when I was six weeks old in April 1940. In this view from Anna's porch, you can see both the gas station on her corner and the store across Massillon Road.

Well I digress once again. On 18 February 1939 my mother, Mildred and my father Charles P Arnold, Sr. who had met in high school, were married at Concordia Lutheran Church by the Reverend J.F. Yount. But just three and a half short years later on 11 August 1942 they were divorced, for reasons never fully understood by me. Mildred took a job as a "Rosie the Riveter" in the hanger at the Akron Municipal Airport. Built in 1929, the hanger, more properly the Goodyear Airdock, which still exists to this day is where the Goodyear Zeppelin Corporation developed and constructed dirigibles, including the famous Akron and Macon, but where versions of the Vought Corsair fighter aircraft were being built between 1942 and 1944. This is where Mildred worked. Her supervisor was a man named William Mains. Now William was just 20 at the time and a little younger than Mildred but the two fell in love quickly and Mildred needed a father for her son. When she told Anna she planned to marry again, Anna asked her about Bill. Mildred answered "he is such a great dancer" to which Anna replied "Well hell Mildred, that does you no good. You don't even dance". Nevertheless, the two were married on 22 August 1942 and Bill moved into the house she and Chuck had bought at 554 Morningview Ave in the Goodyear Heights section of East Akron. Soon thereafter Anna sold her home on Springfield Center Road and moved in with Bill, Mildred, and Charles Jr.

As jobs were plentiful in the growing rubber company industry in Akron, and provided a much better income than teaching, Anna had taken a job in the bead room of the Mohawk Rubber Company, sometime around 1935. She would keep this job until she retired in 1955.

Over the subsequent years Anna would be my tutor and my chauffeur as my mother did not learn to drive until I was practically in college. Anna traveled, visited Elaine and my family often, her niece and husband in Florida yearly, and enjoyed her retirement years. Her past times included listening to Cleveland Indian baseball games on the radio until my parents bought a 7" TV for her to watch these games, later Jeopardy was her favorite show, and then each day she had to work the cross-word puzzle in the paper. She never failed to complete one, even as they progressively became more difficult toward the end of each week and with each passing year. She was never idle. She would sit by the hour crocheting doilies and humming church tunes as my half-brother Edward recalled recently.

And gram had aphorisms for every occasion. If I were misbehaving she might say "do you need a knock on your noggin?" or "Do you need a quick kick in your slats?" I never did quite know where my slats were, but one thing I didn't need was a quick kick there. If she didn't think she looked nice enough she would say "I look like the wreck of the Hesperus" or if I were doing something she didn't think was very important, she would say "Don't piddle around now". When she became tired, it would be "there is no rest for the wicked", or if she were frustrated it would be "fiddle sticks". This former is actually biblical coming from Isaiah 48.28. I must have been near 70 when I came across a collection of Longfellow's poems which included the "Wreck of the Hesperus". Aha! I said surprised, now I know where that came from. Longfellow must have been a favorite of hers for she had memorized "The Song of Hiawatha" as well, which was also in that same collected works of the poet. Edward recalls her saying on occasion "I'll knock you for a row of bent pins". I still haven't found any source for that one. One of Edward's favorite and mine as well was her use of the word "Nertz". I have no idea how she would have spelled this word, but if I were to say something which to her was quite silly she might come back with "you're nertz", or as Edward recalled, if she were to drop her yarn while crocheting, you might hear it. I suspect the derivative of this word is somewhere in the German. In the dictionary it is noted that it was a popular slang word of the late 1930's. Edward recalls that while missing a green light on a snowy hill one winter he heard her exclaim "Oh nertz" as her car slowly slid down the hill to the cross street below.

Anna had a strong and lasting faith in her Lord and remained a member of the Lutheran church until her death. Among the few keepsakes I have from her are a Bible she purchased for me in 1945, a small book of bible stories, and a vacuum tube radio which surprisingly still operates to this day, all from the 40's. She had been living at a home for the elderly in the mid 1970's when she became a victim of a flu epidemic. They closed the home to visitors during this time which my mother was distressed over and complained of in a letter to me. Gram passed away on the 7th of March 1976 at the age of 86. Her last words that my mother could recall were "I'm not feeling very well" as they took her to the hospital. Anna was laid to rest in Mount Peace Cemetery in Akron Ohio.

John Roth and Rosa Wilk

A method I have employed in constructing all the genealogies in this book has been a chronological timeline of events in or related to the individual under study. Along this line I place births, baptisms, census years and events specific to those years, immigration, marriage, deaths, etc.

I started the timeline of Rosa Wilk, maternal grandmother of my wife Elaine, with the birth of her oldest brother Henry, Jr. in 1886 Germany. Henry, Jr. will later emigrate in 1892 with his mother, Kate, and his two younger sisters—Anna, born in Aug 1888 and Rosa, born on 6 October 1890. A 1910 Census entry for Rosie Wilk records 1893 as the year she emigrated. However, her mother Kate in the 1900 Census provided 1892 as the year she and Henry, Jr. emigrated. So 1892 is considered to be more accurate. However, to make things a bit more confusing, both Henry, Sr. and wife Kate provided 1890 as the year of their emigration on the 1910 Census. But since Rosa had been born in late 1890, 1892 remains more accurate in my opinion. Rosa's father Henry, Sr. had emigrated in 1891, according to the 1900 Census which is also considered to be valid.

On July 29, 1883 the Concordia Orphan's home, a very important place in Rosa's life, located in what is now Cabot, Pennsylvania was dedicated and the first house was erected. A school was completed in 1885 and in 1890 a third building was added. Sometime after Rosa's younger sister Marie was born in April of 1894, in the U.S., she, Rosa, and Anna were sent by their father to live in this Lutheran home. It is surmised that following the birth of Rosa's younger brother William, in 1896 and John, in 1898 around the time Marie was 5 years old, Henry, Sr. could no longer support his family and he and his wife decided to send their girls to the home. This is supported in the 1900 Federal Census in which we find Henry, born in November of 1862 and wife Kate, born in November of 1860 living with only their three sons Henry, William, and John and renting rooms in the home of the Backes family at 59 Berry Street in Pittsburgh, while at the same time their three girls were living at the Orphan's home. Still there was another boy, Herman, born in 1902 to 41 year old Kate. In the 1900 Census Kate reported that she had been the mother of 7 children of whom 6 were still alive, the three boys at home and the three girls at the Lutheran Orphan's home. In the 1900 Census taken at the Concordia Orphan's home, the three girls, Anna, Rosalie, and Marie were documented as being residents.

In the next census of 1910 the family was still renting but now living at 62 Berry Street and with the addition of Herman. In this 1910 Census Kate reported that she had been the mother of 10 children of whom 7 were still alive, the four boys at home and the 3 girls still at the Lutheran home. From these two census records we know that one of Kate's children died prior to 1900 or before the census enumeration of 1900. Two more of her children died between the enumeration of 1900 and the enumeration of 1910. But by 1910 it is noted that Henry Sr. had been restricted to his home as he was now in a wheelchair, the surrounding facts of which remain unknown.

On 16 April of 1905, it being Palm Sunday of that year, Rosa was confirmed by Pastor Theo. Andree at Saint Luke's Evangelical Lutheran Church in Hannahstown, Butler Co., Pennsylvania—the same county and close by to where she was living at the Orphan's Home. Rosa was 14 years old at the time and both her Confirmation Certificate and the examination booklet for Communion published in 1887 by her later benefactor Pastor Peter Brand were written in German, the language used in her classes and in church. Her confirmation verse was from the Revelation of St. John 2.10 "Be faithful unto death and I will give you the crown of life". There were 12 teens in her confirmation class. There is also a photo of Rosa and younger sister Marie taken at the time she looked to be of confirmation age and at what certainly appears to be the orchard area of the old Lutheran home (Fig 6), which I and my wife Elaine have visited so many times over the past fifty years.

Eight postcards mailed to Rosa between 15 Feb 1909 when she was 18 years old and 23 Dec 1911 when she was 21 years old help us fill in the events between her confirmation in 1905 and her wedding in 1913. The first post, dated 15 Feb 1909, was signed J.R. considered to have been her future husband John Roth and which simply said "From your Best Frend (sic)". It was addressed in c/o Rev R. Brand, South 18th Street SS (South Side) City. This was probably her first year out of the Orphan's home since she had just turned 18 four months earlier.

Using the 1912 City Directory of Pittsburgh, we find that Rev. Peter Brand resided at 72 S. 18th St on the South Side of Pittsburgh. His church, First Saint Paul's Evangelical Lutheran (LCMS) was located at the corner of 18th and Sidney Streets, a few doors away. A parking lot occupies this spot today.

The second and third posts came on the same day, 17 Sept 1909. Both were postmarked at 1 AM, one with the short note "Dearest Friend Rose . . . . (the remainder difficult to decipher)" was mailed to her address at 1526 Murray Ave East End. This address was most likely the residence of her new employer. The post was signed J. Roth. The other, to Miss Rose Wilk, is difficult to decipher, but was also signed J. Roth. John apparently working a night job would post these cards to Rose on his way home.

The fourth post was dated 23 Sept 1909 to Miss Rose Wilk at 1526 Murray Ave. Pittsburg (Sic), Pa E.E. It is difficult to decipher but is signed J. Roth. The fifth post is signed John and is considered to have been written by her brother. He asks her to wait till he gets home before she marries John. Apparently there was talk of marriage already in 1909. The Sixth postcard was dated 14 Oct 1909 to Miss Rose Wilk at 1526 Murray Ave, East End, City from J. Roth, with the note "Don't forget Sunday evening. I have something important to tell you". The seventh post from J. Roth to Miss Rose Wilk who by this time had a new address of 413 Nobel East End was postmarked 9 Nov 1909. The message—"On my way to work Rose. I Dindent (sic) get a chace (sic) to speak to you the (undeciphered) cut me of (sic) Be sure and let me know went (sic) I will see. This is your frean (sic)".

We learn from the 1910 Census that the home which then 19 year old Rose (Rosie) was living at, 413 Nobel Street, was the residence of the Griffith family (William, a 34 year old Dentist and his 31 year old wife Lydia). It is thought that Rose was caring at that time for the Griffith children, Harold, 2 years old and infant son William, as Rose was listed as a house servant in the Census record.

The final postcard dated 23 Dec 1911 to Rosie Wilk now living at Collins Ave & Broad St (EE or SS) from a friend who had lived with her at the Lutheran home and had just left to be on her own.

Returning to 1900, the Census enumerated on 12 June of that year, reveals that John Roth, 10 years old at the time, was born in May of 1890 and was living at 55 Welsh Way on the South Side of Pittsburgh with his father John, mother Zuzanna, and three younger brothers, William, 6 years old, Rudolph, 4 years old, and Henry, 1 year old. In the same Census it was revealed that John's father John Sr., was born in June 1865 and emigrated from Hungary the same year as his wife in 1886 at age 21. John lived with his family at 55 Welsh Way on the South Side of Pittsburgh where he grew up. His mother, Zuzanna was born in Feb 1870 and as noted emigrated from Hungary in 1886 at the age of 16. She had married John Sr. in 1889, three years after she had emigrated. She had been the mother of 5 children of whom four remained alive in 1900, John and his three brothers. These are my wife's great grandparents on her mother's side.

A map of the South Side of Pittsburgh for the year 1890 clearly shows Welsh Way where John Roth grew up and Sidney and S. 18th Streets where their church, First Saint Paul's Evangelical Lutheran church, was located and where John, it is thought, first met Rosa, sometime around 1909 and began sending her the postcards we have written about.

Ten years later, in the Census of 1910, Zuzanna had changed her name to Susan and there were a few more children in their family—John Jr. was now 20 years old and was reported to have been employed as a shipper in a furniture store (Spear & Co.), William, 16, Rudolph, 4, a new younger brother Walter, 6, Henry, 12, and two new sisters Hilda, 4 and Philomina, 2, both born during the previous decade. The family also had a boarder, Martin Arelt, 33. This boarder is considered to have been Zuzanna's brother as her maiden name according to John and Rosa's marriage license. John Sr. and Susan now report they had emigrated from Germany.

John and Rosa were married by Pastor Peter Brand at their church on 15 October 1913 and from a photo of her taken at the Wieland studio on 913 Boardwalk in Atlantic City, in a then stylish 1913 era bathing suit, it is believed that the couple honeymooned there (Fig 7). In 1914 they were blessed with the birth of twin boys who they named Herbert and Harold. In 1916 they had a girl, who they named Lillian Barbara Rosa Roth, my wife's mother. According to John's draft registration dated 5 June 1917, the family was living at 225 Sterling Street in St. Clair on the South Side. From this record we know that John was born 14 May 1890. He was a tall man of medium build with gray eyes and brown hair when he registered for the draft at age 27.

In the next census of 1920, enumerated on 5 January 1920, we find that both parents are once again reporting they had emigrated from Austria-Hungary. They also report that they have two new daughters—Wilma, age 11 and Elsie, age 8. There is no mention now of Philomina and it is presumed that she must have died during the prior decade. So it would appear that John Junior's mother had 11 children altogether and that two of them, one being Philomina, had died. Meanwhile John Jr. and Rosa were still living at 225 Sterling Street.

On March 27 of 1930 John who was still working at Spear & Co. furniture store in downtown Pittsburgh was crushed by a door in the shipping department where he worked and died shortly thereafter. The census of that year, enumerated on 4 April, just one week after John had died revealed that Rose, now widowed was living on 2524 Diehl Ave., in Carrick, south of the city. Her two boys were now 15 years old and Lillian was 13. Also living with Rose was her younger sister Marie Wilmott, 35 years of age, and recently divorced, and Marie's daughter, Rose's niece, also called Marie, but more affectionately known as Dolly. No one in the household was known to have been employed and it is thought that the money from the settlement of John's death at Spear and Co. was being used to make mortgage payments and buy food and pay bills, though Elaine recalls her grandmother taking odd jobs following John's death, to supplement the family income.

After another ten years had passed, the 1940 Census has both boys now 25 years old working. Harold was a credit clerk at a department store and Herbert, a helper baker at a Stout Bakery. Lillian had married Karl Schuster in 1939 and they were living with Karl's parents in 1940.

Around 1945 Rose and William Kording who attended the same church, Concordia Lutheran (LCMS) in Brentwood were married. William sold or gave the home, that he and his first wife lived in, to his daughter, and moved into Rose's home on Diehl avenue. William, however, died in the late 1950's or early 60's at which time, Rose continued living on Diehl Ave.

In later years when Rose was living with Lillian after her second husband Bart Stocker had passed away, Elaine and I would frequently visit Lillian on Blossom Drive there in Brentwood. Once while Elaine was visiting with our daughter Amy and her infant son Ryan during this period, Norm Schum, a photographer friend of the family took a photo of the five generations—Rose, Lillian, Elaine, Amy, and Ryan (Fig 8). We treasure this photo to this day. Rose would also visit our family as often as possible. While I was pursuing a Master of Science degree in Meteorology at the Pennsylvania State University in State College Pennsylvania, in the early 1970's she came to visit at the age of 80 or 81 to "help" Elaine who by now had three young children of her own, and working atop a footstool, Rose washed windows without batting an eye.

Rose was frequently heard saying "thank you Jesus", particularly after retiring in the evening to her bedroom. This reminded me of Brother Lawrence who was described in the book "The Practice and Presence of God" as one who constantly practiced the presence of God through prayer and meditation. In 1987 she visited us in Upper Marlboro, Maryland to attend our son Charles' high school graduation. And near the age of 96 Rose broke her hip. As her granddaughter Judy tells the story "Mom and Grandma were at the grocery store and upon leaving they saw someone they knew and that person gave Grandma a hug and a kiss. Upon finishing her hug and kiss, Grandma went down on the floor. We often laughed and said, "Wow, what a kiss, it broke grandma's hip"." But with a replacement hip she was able to find the strength to recover and soon walk again, though in early recovery was seen to slide down the steps leading to the ground floor of Lillian's home. As Rose neared 100 she lived out her final years at the same Lutheran home she had come to love as a child. Rose died very peacefully on 4 May 1991 at the age of 100 just 5 months shy of her 101 birthday.

John Clayton and the Electric City Glass Company, Fig 1

Art Glass made by John Clayton, Fig 2

Anna And John Clayton with Daughter Mildred Circa 1918, Fig 3

John Clayton and Jack Clayton's gravesites, Fig 4

The View From Anna's Porch on Springfield Center Road, Fig 5

Rose Wilk and Sister Marie at the Lutheran Orphan's Home Cabot Pennsylvania, Fig 6

Rose Roth Nee Wilk on her honeymoon at Atlantic City Board Walk 1913, Fig 7

Five Generations. Rose sitting with great-great grandson Ryan Mensing, great grandmother Lillian Stocker standing in rear, grandmother Elaine Arnold left, and Mother, Amy Mensing right, Fig 8

Fay Arnold with sons Fred and Charles, Fig 9

Charles Arnold Jr and younger sister Kathy on 3-Wheeler made by his grandfather
Arnold, Fig 10

Fay and Fred Arnold circa 1935, Fig 11

Map of Bavaria Germany, Fig 12

Steerage aboard the Kaiser Wilhelm II Photo by Alfred Stieglitz, Fig 13

The Kaiser Wilhelm II Circa 1904, Fig 14

George Schuster in his Bavarian Uniform Circa 1900, Fig 15

George Schuster with mother and half-sister Circa 1905, Fig 16

Author's visit to Finlay Ohio 1951 with father, grandmother Fay Arnold, half-sister
Marilyn, and half¬-brother David, Fig 17

Perry Garlow's gravesite, Fig 18

Margaret Garlow's gravesite, Fig 19

John Clem, Civil War Drummer Boy for the Union, Fig 20

Family Lutheran Church in Parkentin, Fig 21

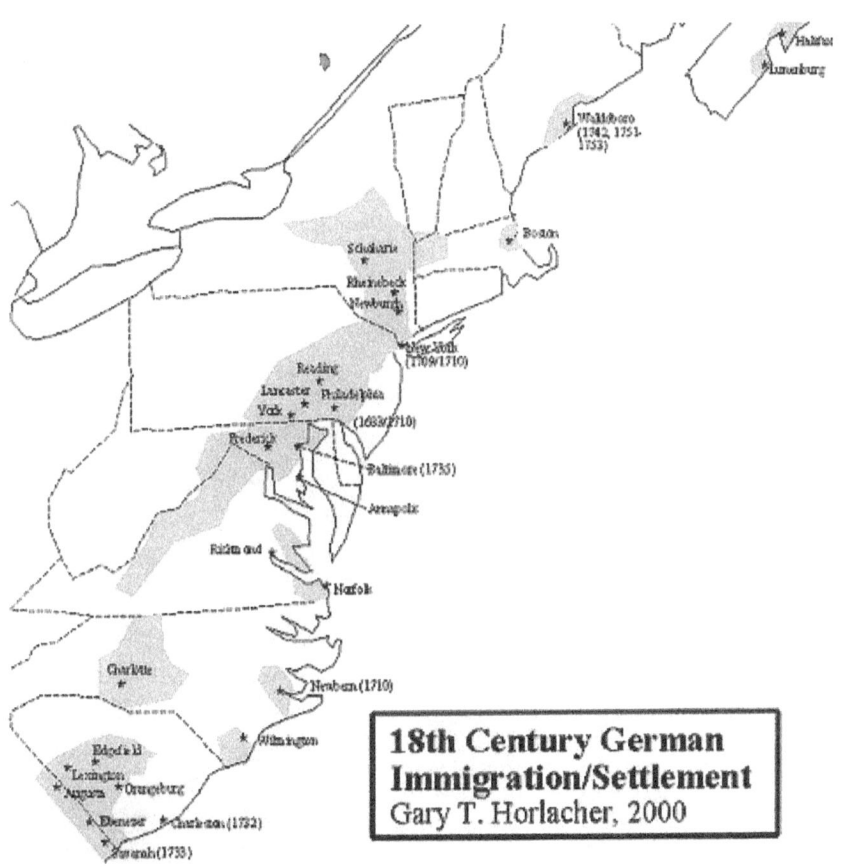

18th Century Immigration & Settlement into Western Maryland, Fig 22

The Author's Family, Fig 23

The Oldest Living Generation of Arnolds and Schusters, Fig 24

Fred Victor Arnold and Fay Marie Garlow

Using City Directories, a marriage record, and the 1940 Census, it was possible to construct the following story of how and where Frederick Victor Arnold and Fay Marie Garlow, my paternal grandparents, met, fell in love, married, and began a family. Fred emigrated from the big city of London, England arriving in the US in 1910 as a young eager 25 year old photographer no doubt with a desire to establish his own photography business in the United States. He had taken up residence in Ocala Florida, a favorite tourist attraction for its Silver Springs River and Glass Bottom boats. Elaine and I visited this spot in the first decade of this new millennium. Both of us had visited Silver Springs as children with our parents and had very fond memories of the glass bottom boat adventure. During this last visit we had our photo taken so the two of us would have a lasting memory of our second visit there.

Although it is not known under what circumstances Fay happened to be in Ocala in August of 1911 since she had just turned 17 at the time and was a small town farm girl from Findlay, Ohio. Was she a tourist on vacation? It would seem unreasonable that her parents would have permitted a girl of 17 to take such a long and un-chaperoned trip on her own. Another unlikely possibility is that she perhaps had run away from home but as we shall learn, she and Fred returned to her hometown of Findlay, Ohio when she most likely needed her mother the most, to be with her when she delivered her first baby. When I wrote her niece in Findlay Ohio in September of 2013 concerning this trip of my grandmother's, she replied that possibly she was with her parents on a vacation visit to Florida where she met Fred and stayed. This seems to be the most likely explanation.

What we do know, however, is that she apparently met Fred there in Ocala after hiring him, it is thought, to take her photo just as her grandson and wife would one day do, a hundred years later. We also know that it would have been a whirlwind romance for this young couple. Within a short period of time the two fell in love and decided to marry. So on 1 August 1911 they were married there in Ocala Florida. During the next several years as we can deduce from the 1913 Tampa City Directories, her and Fred are found living at 1529 7th Ave. Fred's photography business was located in the same city at 1310 Florida Ave. During the spring of this year Fay became pregnant and soon decided to make the trip back north together with Fred to her home town to be with mother and father in Findlay. There on 21 June of 1914 their first son Fred Merrill Arnold was born. These facts are supported by Fred M Arnold's Marriage Record.

During this year Fred Victor was listed in the 1914 Findlay City Directory as a Photographer located on 113 N Main St. Soon thereafter when the family was able to travel, they returned to Florida and took up residence in the city of Jacksonville. Here they lived at 920 W Bay St. while Fred's photography business was conducted at 428 Riverside Ave., according to the 1915 Jacksonville City Directory. Then in the early summer of that year Fay once again became pregnant and on 15 March of 1915 she gave birth to her second son, Charles Perry Arnold (Fig 9), my birth father. His middle name was taken from his grandfather's given name Perry. It now seemed as though the family required a bit bigger home and so by 1916 Charles' birth certificate has his family living at 912 W. Monroe St. in Jacksonville.

After a period of 8 years the family found it necessary to move once again this time back to Ohio. From 1924 on Fred was no longer employed as a photographer but rather a decorator and home painter. His business either dried up or he found it was not enough to support his growing family. Since we know that their first home in Ohio was in East Liverpool, it seems that Fay was not responsible for them having to move. There according to the City Directory of 1924 they lived at 230 Broadway.

During the 1920's Fred became more of an itinerate painter moving to 1557 E Market St. in Akron Ohio from East Liverpool and living there from 1928 to 1931, according to the City Directories for those years. And in 1933 and 1934 they were located at 494 Baldwin Rd in Akron, and finally from the 1940 Census we learn that the family had been living at 1201 Lindsey Ave since 1935 and there I visited these grandparents and came to know a little about each of them—Fred, was to me a stern Englishman. He built me a three wheeled tricycle from metal in short supply during the War years on which I can be seen riding in Figure 10 with my younger sister Kathy holding on for dear life. Fay was a loving grandmother who baked her own bread often taking it hot from the oven cutting me a slice or two, and spreading it with butter and sugar while she tended to the cooking of dandelion greens we had picked together in her small front yard and which she then placed into her pressure cooker. Her and Fred are shown in Figure 11.

George Schuster And Barbara Vogtmann

After months of waiting for additional information while writing this particular story, I finally received a letter in the mail from Ulrike Schwarz, my devoted assistant in Rostock Germany on 19 September 2013. The letter contained a copy of the birth certificate of George Schuster, Elaine's paternal grandfather[2]. George was born in Warmersdorf on 22 January 1881. Where is Warmersdorf? This historically small village is now a section of a larger village called Wachenroth, a town within the Erlangen-Hochstadt district of the German State of Bavaria (See Figure 12). In 1978, this city incorporated Buchfeld, Horbach and Warmersdorf as divisions of the city. Another division of this city is Weingartsgreuth, which is where we find the birth records maintained for Warmersdorf.

George Schuster's mother was Margaretha (or Margaret) Schuster, a young unmarried girl who was having her baby there at home with a midwife, Margaretha Mohning, attending her on the morning she gave birth. The midwife lived ten doors away at house number 18 Warmersdorf while the Schuster residence was at house number 8. While the religion of Ms. Mohning was listed on the birth certificate as protestant, that of Margaret Schuster was surprisingly not listed. Throughout Germany about 65% to 70% of the population are Christians. They are more or less evenly split between the mainstream denominations of Lutheran-Protestantism and Reformed Calvinism united in the EKD (Evangelical Church in Germany) and the Roman Catholic Church. Due to the historical development of religion in Germany, these denominations are concentrated in specific regions.

In the course of the Protestant Reformation and the ensuing Thirty Years' War in the 15th and 16th centuries, religion in Germany ended up being distributed according to the preferences of local rulers: Therefore, most areas in the South or West (especially Bavaria and Northrhine-Westphalia) are Catholic while the North and East are mainly Protestant. This is still pretty much true today. When my wife's father Karl Schuster died in 1968 my mother-in-law gave me a statue and music box of Martin Luther which Karl had purchased at a shop in or near Warmersdorf while visiting his father's birthplace. I learned that the store owner gave it away for a pittance saying that it was of no use to him being catholic. George, however, was born into a Lutheran family and was baptized into the Lutheran faith on 26 Jan 1881.

A year after George was born on 22 January 1881, his mother Margaretha Schuster emigrated to the United States at the age of 23 presumably leaving George in the

---

2   See Table 3 Appendix 1 for a family tree of George Schuster. Note that when his grandparents married in 1867, his mother's family name was legitimized

hands of his grandparents (see footnote 2). In the United States she met and married John Henry Weckesser in 1885. Weckesser had immigrated in 1868 at the age of 23. Then in October of 1886 George's half-sister Anna Katherine Weckesser was born.

When George became 23 years old he too immigrated to the United States arriving aboard the Kaiser Wilhelm II in New York on 8 June 1904. One of the most famous photos of the day was taken by Alfred Stieglitz of the Steerage accommodations aboard the Kaiser Wilhelm as seen in Fig. 13. This ship, shown in Fig. 14 and considered one of the fastest of its day had departed Bremen Germany on 26 May 1904 and after a brief stop in England arrived in New York fourteen days later. George had apparently spent a while as an enlisted Bavarian artillery man during the time of Kaiser Wilhelm der Grosse as seen in Figure 15 in the uniform of that day. This photo was taken at a studio in the city of Wurzburg, 41 miles west of Wachenroth. After arriving in the U.S. he eventually became naturalized on February 9, 1912 in the Western District Court of Pennsylvania.

Barbara Vogtmann was born on May 6, 1876 in Schonbrunn, a village believed to be in the Fichtelgebirge Mountains east of Warmersdorf. Barbara came to the United States aboard the S.S. Munchen arriving in Baltimore, Maryland on June 18, 1889 at the very young and innocent age of 13. She was accompanied by Marga Vogtmann, age 65, and Johann Vogtmann, age 29, thought to have been a grandmother or aunt and an older cousin. They however, are known to have left Barbara at the Port while they journeyed on to Wisconsin. Barbara told my wife Elaine the story of being alone three days before hearing her name being called over a loud speaker and then meeting the Lutheran pastor from Pittsburg, Rev. William Brand, who was sponsoring her. While waiting at the port in Baltimore she would sit by other families with children so as not to be conspicuous. She was a tiny girl with long blond braids and spoke no English which of course made things that much more difficult for her and frightening.

Barbara subsequently met George in Pittsburgh and the two were married on June 10, 1908. She was 31 and he was 28. In 1910 the Federal Census reported that George and Barbara were living at 904 Congress St. in Pittsburgh. The couple had a one year old son George, Jr. We also find that a second family was living with the Schusters— Charles Joestlein, 25 years old and his wife Katherine, 23 years old with 2 year old daughter Helen. From Charles' draft registration for World War I dated 12 September 1918, we know he and Katherine were married on 3 April 1907. An old family photo (Figure 16) shows George Schuster with his mother Margaret Weckesser (nee Schuster) seated, and to her right is Anna Katherine Weckesser who shortly after this photo was taken, married Charles Joestlein.

George died in 1948 but fortunately his DNA was passed along to his descendants. The desire, patience, and whatever other character traits and skills are necessary for one to become a master craftsman were what George passed on. It was first to his son Karl Schuster who built many neighborhood homes south of Pittsburgh, then to his grandson George Schuster, and believed to have also been passed along to his great grandson, Charles P Arnold, III, son of his granddaughter Elaine Schuster.

Barbara lived another six years after George passed away. She died on 19 February 1954. In his last will and testament left to his dearest Baerbel, the nickname he used with Barbara, he wrote "Since I do not know when our good Lord will call me home, and since we have lived together for so many years and have faithfully shared all our joys and sorrows, I would like to remind you of this great love and recommend to you the following" after which he listed suggestions in as kind a German way as possible as to how she should handle his estate.

Great Grand Parents

Perry Commodore Garlow and Margaret Nee Heines

MY EARLIEST RECOLLECTION of Findlay, Ohio is a visit with my grandmother Fay Arnold after grandfather Fred had passed away in 1949. She had returned to the home of her late parents to live with her sister Emma. It was 1951 and I was 11 at the time and I was along with my father and his wife Anna and my two half siblings, David and Marilyn on a trip from Akron to Findlay to visit my grandmother. I have photos taken of me with her in the driveway of the home she was then living in with her sister Emma, while I was on that visit. Here I am in Figure 17 with my grandmother, my birthfather, and my half-siblings.

While engaged in the research for this branch of my family, I serendipitously found the name of one Dorthey Garlow in the autumn of 2007 living in Findlay. Hoping she may be a related Garlow I wrote Ms. Dorthey explaining that I was engaged in some family history and was searching for information about the parents of my paternal grandmother, Perry and Margaret Garlow. I asked if she were related and if so, could we please correspond. I had to wait only a matter of days before I received my first letter from then 84 year old Dorthey. She replied that yes indeed we were related and that her father, Fred Garlow, and my grandmother, Fay Arnold, were brother and sister. This made Dorthey and me first cousins once removed. Her grandparents and my great grandparents were indeed Perry and Margaret Garlow.

Later that year after exchanging several letters I learned that my high school class of 1958 was having its reunion in the following summer of 2008. Since Akron

58

is only a few hours east of Findlay, I made plans for Elaine and me to attend the reunion and then travel on to Findlay to meet Dorthey, other cousins of mine in the city, visit cemetery gravestones, take pictures, and collect other genealogical related information on this side of my family. This information together with what I have gleaned from the internet search sites became the basis for this short vignette.

Perry Commodore Garlow had become the namesake for my father's middle name which in turn became my middle name. Perry was born on 22 February of 1851, the same year as the American gunfighter Commodore Perry Owens, but I believe it is more likely that he had been named in honor of Commodore Oliver Hazard Perry (23 August 1785-23 August 1819) who was regarded as a true American hero. Commodore Perry served in the U.S. navy during the war of 1812 and had earned the title of "Hero of Lake Erie", for having won a decisive battle against all odds with the British in the Battle of Lake Erie. The United States Navy recognizes 13 October 1775 as the date of its official establishment but with the end of the American Revolutionary War, the Continental Navy was disbanded. Under President George Washington threats to American merchant shipping by pirates in the Mediterranean led to the Naval Act of 1794, which created the U.S. Navy. Six frigates were authorized as part of this Act. Over the next 20 years, the Navy fought the French Navy in the Quasi-War (1798-99), the Barbary States of North Africa in the First and Second Barbary Wars, and the British in the War of 1812. Perry was in the news throughout the first five decades of the 19th century and there is little doubt in my mind that he became the influence behind the naming of many young males of that day and age, as well as places, counties, and towns throughout the country.

In the Census of 1860[3] enumerated on the 20th of July of that year we find Perry Garlow living with his parents in Thorn Township, Perry County, Ohio, named incidentally for Commodore Oliver H. Perry. Perry was the youngest of the four children born to Catherine in Pennsylvania. His siblings included two older sisters, Amada, age 17 and Elvira, age 15 and an older brother, John who was 28 during the year of this census. Catherine was 43 years old when Perry was born in February of 1851. In this census Perry was 9 years old and his mother was 52.

Perry's wife Margaret was born the seventh of nine children on 29 December 1853 in Pulaski Township, Williams County, the most north western county in Ohio[4]. Her

---

[3]   The 1860 Federal Census was the first census to enumerate the names of all family members of a household.

[4]   Elsewhere it has been recorded that Margaret was one of twelve children born to John and Catherine Heines. See http://genforum.genealogy.com/himes/messages/924.html

parents, my second great grandparents, were John and Catherine (Nee Ritter) Heines[5] who were married on 5 March 1840 in Boliver, Tsucarawas County, Ohio. John was one of 9 children born to George and Catherine (nee Musser) who were married in 1815, my third great grandparents. George had emigrated with his parents from Germany and settled in Pennsylvania, later migrating to Tuscarawas County, Ohio, near Boliver. In the years before they were married Perry had moved with his parents from Pennsylvania to southeast Ohio and finally into northwest Ohio. Meanwhile, in the intermediate years, Margaret had grown up and remained in Williams County without moving.

Soon after the death of his mother Catherine, Perry moved with his father Peter from Perry County in the south east corner of Ohio to the north western most county of the state where he would meet Margaret. I believe the couple soon fell in love and were married on the 7th of August 1873. It is interesting to note that he spelled his last name Garloch on their marriage certificate.

Many details of their life together have been lost between the year they married and 1900 when they were still found living in Williams County, Ohio. This does tell us however, that Perry did not have the wanderlust of his parents and had become content with farming and raising children, for in the 1900 Census year, Margaret reported she had given birth to ten children of whom ten were still living. Only six were listed however. William, age 16, followed by Alice, age 14, followed by Jacob, age 11, Freddie, age 9, my grandmother Fay, age 5, and her sister Ruth, age 3.

Ten years later in 1910 the family was still living in Pulaski Township, Williams County, with Freddie, Fay, and Ruth still single and living at home. Daughter Estelle had married Earl McCaslin by this time and they were living with Perry and Margaret. Perry was 59 now and Margaret was 56.

Finally, by 1920, the couple now 69 and 66 years old had moved into Marion Township, Hancock County, Ohio just 5 miles east of Findlay. Their son Freddie, now going by Frederick and his wife Edith, 28 and 25 years old respectively and their two children ages 2 and a half and 1 and a half were living with the elderly Garlows. Then in 1924 at the age of 74 and 4 months Perry died on the 27th of the month. Margaret would go on to live another 15 years, dying at the age of 86 on 7 May 1939. Both are buried in Maple Grove Cemetery in Findlay Ohio, Hancock County (Figs 18 and 19). While visiting this cemetery in 2008 I found next to Perry's gravestone a marker that reads GAR Veteran—the Grand Army of the Republic. Perry had evidently been a veteran of the Civil War and served in the Union Army. In

---

[5] Himes has been spelled in various ways including Heines, Hines, etc.

August of 2013 I found another cousin, Tim Garlow who lives in Orange California. Tim's mother had told him she recollected the family story that Perry had served as a drummer boy with the Union Army. If it were true then Perry would join the ranks of such boys as John Clem and would have looked much like Clem as pictured in Fig 20. Musicians on the battlefield were drummers and buglers, with an occasional fifer. Buglers had to learn forty-nine separate calls. These ranged from battle commands to calls for meal time. Some of these required musicians were drummer boys not even in their teens, which allowed an adult man to instead be a foot soldier. The most notable of these under aged musicians was John Clem, also known as "Johnny Shiloh". Drummers would march to the right of a marching column. Similar to buglers, drummers had to learn 39 different beats: fourteen for general use, and 24 for marching cadence.

Perry's Son Fred had registered with his local draft board on 5 June 1917 when he was 26 years old, perhaps knowing of his father's service to the Union Army, but in the 1930 Fed Census he provided evidence that he had not been given the opportunity to serve in the military.

Ferdinand Karnuth and Wilhelmina Anna Maria Gastmeier

I have this wonderful old picture which is displayed proudly on the wall of family photos in our home south of Washington D.C. It is of Ferdinand and Wilhelmina Karnuth with their five children, Amelia, Henry, Fred, Anna, and William. I believe it was taken around 1913 or possibly a bit earlier. Sometime after Anna, my grandmother, had completed college in Buffalo and before or possibly just after she had married John Clayton. She has a ring on her finger and she looks to be about 21 which suggests the year. All seven people are handsome. I've been told by my children though, that their great-great grandmother looks uncannily like Jonathon Winters, while Ferdinand with his wonderful handlebar mustache looks suspiciously like Geraldo Rivera.

As we shall learn more about in a later story, Minnie, the knick-name for Wilhelmina, was born on 10 Dec 1865 in the small village of Hohenfelde, in the far northern modern State of Mecklenburg-Vorpommern, Germany just a few miles south of the Baltic Sea. She was baptized on 24 December 1865 at the Evangelical Lutheran Church in nearby Parkentin. This church, originally built in the 1100's is where birth, baptism, and confirmation records for her and other members of our family are maintained. The cemetery next to it as seen in Figure 21 is where members of this same family have been buried. Although we do not know for sure, we believe that Ferdinand was also from that same village. But if not from that same village then most likely from Mecklenburg as he reported in the 1880 Federal Census that he had emigrated from Prussia. Minnie had immigrated in 1882 according to the 1900 census when she was 17, together with her mother Maria and step-father August Stier, brother Martin Gastmeier age 8, and two Stier children, Paul Karl Wilhelm, born 23 November 1878 and daughter Friedrike Christiane Dorothea, born 23 July 1880. With help from Ulrike Schwarz I found that they all departed on 15 October of 1882 aboard the Vandalia, a ship belonging to the famous Hamburg-American Line, the first German transatlantic steamship line established in 1847. They arrived on 3 November 1882 at Ellis Island.

Ferdinand immigrated 10 years earlier in 1872 according to the same census, although in the 1925 New York State Census mentioned in the story of Anna and John Clayton, it is reported he immigrated in 1879 and it was to Buffalo he had come. We also know that his parents had immigrated, for his mother Caroline Karnuth Nee Hüpke was listed as a witness to several of his children's baptisms. Regardless of the exact date of his immigration, we know that his naturalization documents were filed on 8 Feb 1880 and approved on 27 Feb 1882. These actions appear to support the 1879 year of immigration. Still, he must have met Minnie very soon after she had emigrated as they were married in 1883. From the census of 1900 the couple was living in Olean on Buffalo Street next to her daughter Maria. Minnie was 35 years old and all five of their children, mentioned above, had been born and were living with them. A baptismal certificate for Ferdinand Heinrich Ernst Karnuth, son of Ferdinand and Minnie gives a birthdate of 4 October 1887 and a baptismal date a month later on 6 November. This son must have died soon thereafter as Fred (my great uncle Fritz who was so good at his spittoon) was born a year later on 26 Sept 1888.

From the 1900 Federal Census Ferdinand's birthdate was October 1853, so he would have been 46 in June of 1900 when the census was enumerated. If he had immigrated in 1872 he would have been 19 years old at the time and 29 the year the two married. Minnie would have been 18 when she married. He was listed in this census as being a laborer. We know from other sources that his occupation was that of a gardener who worked with improving yards and landscaping them.

Although we have no explicit reason why, the couple had moved to Akron, Ohio by 1928 according to an Akron City Directory of that year. They had made their home at 824 Walsh Ave. Two of their children were also listed in this directory, including great uncle Fritz, who had married my aunt Evelyn. This couple was living at 359 Welch Ave. Fritz was working at Mohawk Rubber Co. His brother Henry with his wife Helen was also listed. Henry was working with the B&O Railroad Co. and this couple was living at 795 Evans Ave. Both Henry and Fritz had been living in Akron since at least 1926 according to that years city directory. I feel as if it were the lure of the Rubber companies and the security of a pension with them that drew many to Akron in that day and age. And fortunate were they all to have jobs, for in just four short years the great depression would tear apart the financial strength of America. Anna of course was still married to John and living in Olean as we recall from their story, but by late in 1931 would join this part of her family in Akron. As an interesting sidebar to this story, I found both a Mildred W Clayton, my mother's maiden name, in the 1926 Directory, though she was only 9 years old living with her mother in Olean at the time, as well as an Anna Clayton working at the Mohawk Rubber Co., both spurious and of no connection to my family, but even stranger things occur while doing genealogical research.

The Olean Evening Times reported that Ferdinand died on 22 May 1931, having died at the age of 78. Minnie was to die 8 years later on 13 Oct 1939, 5 months before I was to be born. She died at age 74.

A Sidebar Vignette

Great Uncle Jacob Garlow the Oilman from Bakersfield

M Y GREAT UNCLE on my father's side was Jacob Garlow He left his small Midwest home in Findlay Ohio where he was born on Nov 29 1888, sometime in the early 1900's, and moved to Bakersfield California and lived there at a home on 1226 Pacific Street. Before the start of World War I and the great depression, Jacob married a beautiful Italian girl named Amelia Mae Monotti from Bakersfield. Amelia like Jake came from a large family, hers having 11 children. They were married on 24 January 1913 at a Baptist Church in Bakersfield. Together they had two boys, Jake G Garlow Jr. and Robert Garlow. Jacob soon became a wealthy oil man working for Stockton Oil Co. and other oil companies around the globe. These included the Burma Oil Company of Scotland, the Honolulu Oil Company, and the Oceanic Oil Company from which he retired in 1959. He traveled the globe widely in search of oil in such places as Angola, Africa, Burma and elsewhere. A story is told that when the couple lived in Burma they had a servant one of whose jobs it was to check for any snakes that may have spent the night near the front door of their home.

When Jake retired he had a home built for him and Amelia in Morro Bay, California on a hill overlooking the bay of the Pacific Ocean. The couple vacationed in faraway countries such as Hong Kong and Rotterdam while traveling first class aboard such ships as the S.S. President Coolidge and the Dutch ship S.S. Rijndam. After a long and very successful life, Jacob died on 1 February 1970 at the age of 81, three months after his wife of 56 years had pre-ceased him on 5 November 1969. Both are buried there in Bakersfield at the Union Cemetery, Plot 1357-3.

In 1984 when we moved from California to Maryland never having heard of Jacob Garlow we left our eldest daughter Amy there to finish College. Amy eventually found a teaching job and where might you suppose it was located? You guessed it— Bakersfield, where she married and had 3 children all the while not knowing about her great-great uncle Jacob. There are still Garlows in Bakersfield to this day in 2013 and perhaps one day we will meet some more distant Garlow cousins as we did in Findlay in 2008 and as I have since found in 2013 south of Bakersfield in Orange County California.

*"Respect for our ancestors elevates
the character and improves the heart"*

Daniel Webster

Second Great Grandparents

Peter and Catherine Garlow

THIS STORY IS about my second great grandparents, Peter and Catherine Garlow[6], the large family of 11 children they started as young teenage parents in the mid 1820's, where they most likely met, where they lived over the next 50 years, and the early pioneering spirit they both must have felt at a time when the country was first beginning to move west beyond the Appalachians. Lewis and Clark had just completed their great expedition to the Pacific and returned in late September of 1806 and the news of their adventure was beginning to spread. The story of Peter and Catherine, however, will by necessity be mixed with stories of their fathers and grandfathers, as they too began their own adventure.

In the third U.S. census conducted in 1810, John Garlough, believed to be my 3rd great grandfather is listed among the residents of Linton Hundred Township of Washington County, located in far western Maryland. Only the head of household was named in this census. Members of the household are listed by age group and sex not by name. His age is in the over 26 under 45 bracket. His wife is also in the same age bracket. He has 2 sons and 4 daughters. He owned no slaves. One of his two sons

---

[6]   The original German spelling of Garlow is believed to have been Garloch, but variations include Garlock, Garlough, and Garlow, which is the common spelling used in our family today.

was in the under age 10 bracket and is believed therefore to have been my 2nd great grandfather Peter Garlow born in 1805.

In this same census of 1810 John Garlough is listed along with two brothers, Christopher (or Christian), who had 4 boys and 5 girls, and Jacob the youngest of the three, in age bracket over 16 under 26, and who had one daughter in the less than 10 age bracket. Although three of Christopher's sons were under 10 years of age of which one could have been my 2nd great grandfather Peter, I remain convinced it was John who was Peter's father since Peter would later in life name his firstborn son John presumably after his father John or even after his grandfather, my 4th great grandfather John Garloch[7].

From the Garloch-Elliott family tree and the history of this family name as found on the internet we read that John Garloch, whom I believe may well have been my 4th great grandfather, was of either Jewish German descent or of Gentile German descent. He and his son's families arrived in Washington County, Maryland well before 1790, because his name shows up on that year's census, the first U.S. Census, as well as an earlier Maryland census of 1778. Figure 22 shows a map of 18th century German immigration and settlement along the east coast. In Maryland one can see how this settlement extended westward into Preston County, West Virginia. John Garloch's family along with his son John Garlough appears on the 1800 census. His four children, John, Christopher (possibly Christian), Elizabeth, and Christina were also born in Germany, according to this Garloch-Elliott family tree, but has not been confirmed independently. Elizabeth was most likely married by 1810 and for that reason was not found as a Garlough at that time. John Garloch did not appear on the 1810 census as he had died there in Washington County, Maryland in 1804, a year before his grandson Peter Garlow was born.

I surmise that in 1810, John Garlough would have been near 50 years old, so that when he immigrated around 1778, he would have been 18 years of age or younger. We also learn from this Garloch-Elliott family tree that his wife's name was Margaret. And again according to this same family tree, John died in 1838 in Richland township, Belmont County, Ohio along the Ohio River not far from where, as we shall learn, his son Peter and daughter in law Catherine Garlow moved sometime after 1851. Since he was recorded in the 1830 census as living in Belmont County and listed as being of 60 and under 70 years of age, he must have been near 70 in 1830 if and only if the Garloch-Elliott tree is accurate.

---

[7]   See Coda for more extensive consideration of my 3rd, 4th, and 5th great grandfathers, all John Garlochs.

Historically we know also that a large group of the settlers of Washington County in the late 1700's were Palatines or members of German royalty, but we have no evidence that John Garloch, was among this class of immigrants. German Immigrants landed at Annapolis and later some at Baltimore. From there they traveled over the bad roads of the time to their destinations in far western Washington County.

Now Peter Garlow, was born in the Linton Hundred division of Washington County which, noted earlier, was located in far western Maryland in 1805. In the early 19th century, tax records for Washington County were ordered by Hundred, a term that referred to civil divisions with counties, whereas in England hundreds were supposed to contain one hundred families, one hundred freemen or one hundred manors, it was only used as a civil term in Maryland. Piecing together information extracted from the Federal Census records from 1810 to 1860 it was possible to develop the following two scenarios to explain where Peter could have met his wife Catherine.

In the 1820 Census there was a John Garloch living in German Township, Fayette County, Pennsylvania. His age was between 16 and 25. He was living with his wife and children: two males under 10 years of age, 1 male 10 to 15 years of age (who in this scenario we have made John's younger brother Peter Garlow), one female under 10 years of age, and two females between 16 and 25 (one of which would have been his wife). In this scenario John Garloch, as I have speculated, is supposed to have been Peter Garlow's older brother and the son of John Garlough who was listed as being between 26 and 44 in the 1810 Federal Census with a son 10 through 15. John Garlough in 1820 would have been between 36 and 54 but is believed to have died resulting in his son John moving with Peter and his other siblings to Fayette County, Pennsylvania. Or as explained in the Garloch-Elliot family tree, John Garlough could have moved on to Belmont County Ohio by 1830.

Continuing with this scenario, Peter would have met and married Catherine there in German Township between 1820 and 1824. Their eldest child, a daughter, is known to have been born no later than 1825. By 1830 this family had moved 10 miles south into Preston County, Virginia (prior to the Civil War), most likely into the Grant District which lay immediately south of Fayette County and immediately west of Linton Hundred across the Maryland line. Some support is added to this scenario in the fact that Catherine reported in later census records that she had been born in Pennsylvania.

In the second scenario Peter moves separately to Preston County while his older brother John moved with his own children (all of which could have been under 10 years of age) to German township after their father died prior to 1820, or had moved on to Ohio. From **A History of Preston County West Virginia Part One** written in

1913[8], we find it stated that Catherine (Nee Cuppett) married Peter Garloch. Kate, as she was called, was the tenth child of John (1774-1855) and Susanna Cuppett (Nee Spahr), the daughter of Frederick Spahr.

John and Susanna Cuppett, are my third great grandparents and are recognized as being pioneers of Preston County[9]. John, born December 4, 1774 and lived till August 20, 1855[10], moved from Bedford County, Pennsylvania in 1808 at the age of 34, the year Catherine was born, and became a tavern owner along the "Mud Pike". This road connected travelers in the Grant district of Preston County with the National Road. Cuppett's stone tavern was located a mile east of the Glade Farms Post Office. Glade Farms remains to this day an unincorporated community in Preston County. It is located on West Virginia Route 26 some 6 miles north-northeast of Brandonville. The following description of this tavern is provided in the above referenced History. "*This house bore the name of being haunted. Uncanny tales are related of the invisible beings that frequented it by night and made the hours of darkness miserable to the stranger.*" John lived to be 80 years old and at least one of his daughters, Mary, lived to be 87.

Catherine's brothers all did very well for themselves. Parson B. Cuppett became a Methodist preacher, while his brother John H. became a merchant of Clarksburg. Charles H. was a principal of city schools. John T. and Victor became business men in Pennsylvania. David E., a graduate of the State University became an attorney and member of the State Legislature.

John Cuppett's father-in-law, Frederick Spahr who died in 1835 and also recognized as a Preston County pioneer was the author's fourth great grandparent and a frontier doctor who acquired some of his medical lore from "*the Red men of the forest*" according to the Preston History cited above. On 2 September 1843, The Cuppett Lutheran Church was organized in the Grant District. The church deacon was Daniel Cuppett eldest son of John and Kate Cuppett who along with sons John, Jacob, and Henry were members of the church.

But I digress. In this second scenario, I believe Peter met and married Catherine there in the Grant District of Preston County between 1820 and 1824. The 1830

---

8 By Oren F. Morton, copyright 1913 Page 425. See also History of Preston County (West Virginia) by S.T. Wiley, 1882.

9 See footnote 6 above page 425

10 These dates for John and Susannah Cuppett are based on *http://trees.ancestry.com/tree/ 6545436/photo/FlwtTaKx863PnboLJ_Zyn4nDsVwPIqzF6pNSh4gXrSexxcxdaSpYELicnJLeZtjy/ 500*

Census has this young family still residing in Preston County with two young girls. Sometime after 1830 the family moves, most likely using the "Mud Pike" road to Uniontown, Fayette County, Pennsylvania. Perhaps this move was made to be closer to Peter's older brother John who would by then have been anywhere from 40 to 45 years old. There were also Cuppetts who lived in and around Uniontown at the time. So in the 1840 Census the family is living there in Uniontown, Pennsylvania.

In the 1850 Census the family is found to have moved from Uniontown to German Township just 8 miles west but still in Fayette Co., Pennsylvania. This census now provides names of household members together with their ages. Peter is 45, Catherine is 43. Daughter Susan is now 18. She was listed in the 1840 census as the one daughter who was 5 to 10 years old. William, their son is 16. His occupation is given as being a farmer. This is the second of two sons listed in 1840 as being between 5 and under 10 and who was actually 6 years old at the time having been born in 1834. We will discover in a moment who the second son was. A daughter Elizabeth, 13 years old, is the daughter who in 1840 was listed as being less than 5 years of age. Of the two youngest girls born in the 1820's, one would now be under 25 and the other would be of 25 and under 30. So it is supposed that both these women were now married and gone from home. And then there are Amanda and Elvira, 7 and 6, born in 1843 and 1845 respectively and who are also named in the 1860 Census. Between 1825 when their eldest daughter was born and 1851 when Perry, their youngest was born, Peter and Catherine had 10 children, 4 sons and 6 daughters' altogether. I also found it curious in the 1850 Census that Peter now spells his last name as "Garlaugh" for the first time. He still lists his occupation as that of a carpenter.

By 1860, Peter's brother most likely had died, and so the family has decided to move westward, no doubt packing all their belongings and children into a Jersey wagon, famous in its time, and setting out on the National Road from German Township, Pennsylvania to Wheeling Virginia and there crossing the Ohio River by Ferry and continuing on the National Road which crossed through Belmont County and into Thorn Township, Perry Co., in south eastern Ohio along the Ohio River valley, where they settled. Perry County was first settled by Pennsylvania Germans in the early 1800's and would therefore have provided a comfortable new environment for the German Garlows. The county is named in honor of Commodore Oliver Hazard Perry, a hero of the Battle of Lake Erie in 1813, during the War of 1812, as noted earlier.

Recall from the 1840 Census that Peter had two sons between 5 and 10 years of age. Recall also that one of those sons was found in 1850 to be William who was 16 and by 1860 was 26. Well William's older brother in that earlier age group turns out to have been John Garlow who we now find to be 28 years old, having been born in 1832. It is the authors opinion that John, not mentioned in the 1850 census had moved to Ohio shortly before that time and had established a home in Thorne Township and had become a farmer. His father, 55, and mother, 52, were in 1860 getting along in age and it is supposed that they were encouraged by John to move West and live with him and that is why we now find John listed along with his father Peter, named as head of the house, and his mother. His two sisters, Amanda and Elvira are also found living with their brother John and their parents. Amanda is now 17 and Elvira has just turned 16. William, their younger brother, who was listed as a farmer back in Pennsylvania during the 1850 Census is believed to have moved further westward into Williams County Ohio. Then shortly after the 1860 census Catherine died on 28 Sept 1861 at the age of 53 and was buried in the Lutheran Reformed Cemetery in Perry County. Shortly thereafter Peter moved to Pulaski Township in Williams county Ohio to live with his son William. And it was there that he died on April 2, 1877 at the age of 73 at the home of his son William. His obituary says he died of a disease of the liver.

There were four Union soldiers by the name of William Garlow. The most likely to have been the son of Peter Garlow belonged to the 16th regiment, US Infantry (Regular Army). If we can show at some point that this William was Perry's brother William, then both he and Perry served in the Union Army. It should also be noted that the family surname is once again spelled Garlow, no doubt according to John's wishes.

Catherine had given birth to her last child in 1851 at the age of 43. This was Perry Commodore Garlow, my great grandfather who we read of earlier. All four of these children, John, Amada, Elvira, and Perry were born in Uniontown, Pennsylvania. When Perry's son Jacob of whom we read of in the previous story applied for his passport in 1919, he listed his father's birthplace as Uniontown in agreement with that city listed as the birthplace for these four children in the 1860 census.

Peter as we noted above died on 2 April 1877 at the home of his son William. Peter was buried in Fountain Grove Cemetery in Bryan, Williams County, Ohio. His gravestone has the year of his death as 1875. But since his son William and William's wife Ruth were buried in the same plot 43 years later when the gravestone was probably set it seems likely this is how the incorrect date was engraved on the stone. Catherine as we have noted died in Thorn Township, Perry County Ohio in 1861. She was 53 years, 4 months, and 27 days old when she died and was buried in the Lutheran Reformed Cemetery there in Thorn Township.

Maria Anna Gastmeier And The Day Laborer

Many years ago, perhaps as many as 40 my mother gave me an old German document. My Grandmother Anna had just passed away and would have been able to translate the old German script but since I was unable to, I simply filed it along with other genealogical data and didn't return to it until a few years ago. Even then, I found I was able to translate only a few words such as the two names Wilhelmine Anna Maria and Maria Anna Gastmeier, a date of 1865 December 10, abschrift or copy at the top of the single page, and a date of 19 July 1882 at the bottom of the page. The copy showed that the original had a seal from Doberan.

My great grandmother's married name was Wilhelmine Anna Maria Karnuth and her mother's name was Mary Stier. From census documents and baptismal certificates, and the help of Ulrike Schwarz in Rostock, Germany, I was able to determine that Mary Stier was Maria Anna Gastmeier, born on July 11 1843 in the village of Althof, (also known as Zwilling?). At the same time her twin brother, Johann Carl Friedrich was born. She and her brother were baptized on 11 December 1843 in the Lutheran church in Parkentin. A second brother, Joachim Christoph Martin Gastmeier was born 8 June 1849 in Althof. He was baptized 8 December 1849.

From everything else I knew, I concluded quite naturally that Maria was married and that her husband, I assumed was an unknown, at that point in time, Mr. Gastmeier. Furthermore I believed he had died in Germany and she remarried August Stier in 1878, according to the 1900 Fed Census, and the couple immigrated to the United States in 1882. From the same Census record I found that both Wilhelmine and a Martin Gastmeier, who had been born in 1874, had immigrated with them together with children whose last names were Stier. I was still thinking that Gastmeier died shortly after the birth of his son Martin and that Maria met Stier sometime in the ensuing 4 years and the two decided to get married. I also came across Wilhelmina's daughter Amelia's death certificate which had been signed by Amelia's daughter Gertrude. It listed Wilhelmina's maiden name as Gosmire, not knowing, I surmised, that it was a misspelling of her father Gastmeier. This seemed to confirm that her father had died in Germany and that the new family then decided to immigrate.

Meanwhile I continued to attempt to find someone who could translate this old document of mine.

Then in early June of 2013 while looking for more information about Maria Anna Gastmeier's husband who I continued to believe had died in Germany, I found a Gastmeier family tree on line. Thinking it may be of help in identifying the long dead second great grandfather I sought contact with the lady whose family tree it was a part of. This was Ulrike Schwarz, a professional Genealogist whom I mentioned above. She lives in the city of Rostock, Germany just a few miles south of the Baltic Sea and was very eager to be of help to me. I soon received a copy of her family tree, which while, unfortunately, proving not to be of any help, did prompt me to ask her if she would be willing to translate my document. She agreed and I emailed her a scanned copy.

Within a day I received her reply. I was both astonished and somewhat dismayed at what I learned. Wilhelmine Anna Maria it turned out, was the illegitimate daughter of Maria Anna Gastmeier and the father was simply listed as a "day laborer". She had been born in the villiage of Hohenfelde, a few miles to the west of Rostock. The date of 10 Dec 1865, was Wilhelmine's birthdate. And another date embedded in the text of the document gave her baptismal date of 24 Dec 1865. The document stated that it had become the birth and Baptismal register of the local church books. It was signed and dated 19 July 1882 by a pastor Karsten. Besides this information, Ulrike also sent me a scanned copy of the confirmation register for Wilhelmine dated 21 March 1880.

While this clarified things a little better for me, it left some lingering questions— Martin Gastmeier for one. He was born 9 years after Wilhelmine in 1874. I was also to learn that at the church in Parkentin, that Maria Anna had no further children baptized with the name Gastmeier. Had Maria Anna been promiscuous for nearly a decade, I wondered? I really did not want to accept this as the only possible explanation, especially given she had Wilhelmine baptized in 1865, confirmed in 1880 and registered this birth and baptism with the church in 1882. The fact that this registration was done at this time is considered to have been in preparation for their emigration in that same year. Maria would have to show that her daughter's birth had been duly registered with the Lutheran church back in Germany before they could enter the U.S. But as far as Martin Gastmeier is concerned he was listed on the ship's manifest as Wilhelmine's brother when they sailed for America.

Then in another email from Ulrike Schwarz I learned further details about their journey to America as reported in my earlier story about Wilhelmine's mother Anna. I found that they all departed on 15 October of 1882 aboard the Steamship Vandalia and arrived on 3 November 1882. Ulrike also confirmed that it was not the August Stier from Vorbeck I thought it may have been but rather August Joachim Theodore Stier from Hohenfelde, Germany who married Anna Gastmeier on 31 May 1878. And this man's birth year was approximated to be 1850.

In the course of time I learned that Maria Anna Gastmeier was born to Johann Friedrich Gastmeier and Anna Maria Dorothea (Nee Schröder) who married on 25 November 1836 at the community church in Mulsow. These were now known to be my 3rd great grandparents on my mother's side. Johann Gastmeier was born in the village of Kamin in 1806 and died in Hohenfelde on 3 June 1878, just 3 days after his daughter Maria married August Stier. He was not buried until 3 September 1878 at the church in Parkentin.

Coda

T HERE WERE AT least three questions which were left unanswered in the previous pages. One has to do with the question of why did my grandparents or my wife's grandparents emigrate when they did? What were the underlying factors which influenced them? I want to examine these questions in the closing section of this book. I also want to try and make sense of who the father and grandparents of my second great grandfather Peter Garlow was. Finally, there remains the question of what happened to the brother of my great grandmother Karnuth, Martin Gastmeier.

Why did our grandparents decide to leave Germany and England when they did? Although we will never know the exact or most compelling reasons, for each of the individuals, we do know a great deal about conditions in Germany which encouraged emigration from there in the 1870's through the first decade of the new century. While 2 grandparents emigrated in 1873, 1 emigrated in 1878, 2 in 1882, 1 in 1889, 1 in 1893, 1 in 1904 and the last to emigrate was in 1910.

These were years of great emigration from Germany. From an 1893 report published by the Royal Commission on Labor[11], we know that between Bismark's appointment as minister president of Prussia in 1862 and his departure from office in 1890, almost 3 million Germans left their country in search of a better life abroad. Many of them chose to enter the United States. This report is important to the individuals reported in the above vignettes as it reveals that the two main districts from which there had been

---

[11]   Source: Royal Commission on Labor, Foreign Reports: Germany, London, 1893, pp. 98-99.

emigration were the southwest and the northeast, the two major regions of Germany from which the Karnuths and the Schusters are known to have lived, the Karnuths from Prussia and the Schusters from Bayern. In the southwest, the population had begun to outgrow both the land supply and the supply of supplementary employment; in the northeast it had become increasingly difficult for a day laborer on one of the great estates to emancipate himself from his state of servitude. It had become impossible to acquire the money to purchase even by years of saving, a small plot of land.

One of the most difficult and perplexing problems in establishing the Garlow branch of my family tree was finding the father of Peter Garlow. For example the Federal Census records for 1800, 1810, and 1820 contain four John Garlow's[12]. These four are all believed to be father-sons. On the 1800 Census for Linton Hundred, Washingon County, Maryland there are two John Garloch Jr's! The first, identified by the letter A in Table 1 has 1 son under 10 years of age. There are two males between 26 and 44 years of age, and one male 45 and over. This last male I believe is John Garloch Sr. and have designated him by the letter C. In the Maryland, Compiled Census and Census Substitutes Index 1772-1890 available in Ancestry.com, we find a John Garlock living in Washington County in 1778, 12 years before the first Federal Census of 1790. Were he 23 years old at that time he would have been in the 45 and over age bracket in 1800, which is the age bracket where C was found to be listed.

The second John Garloch Jr., 4 names below the first John Garloch Jr. is 16 through 25 years of age and has 3 daughters under 10. I have designated him by the letter B. I believe A is the father of B and the son of C. Furthermore I believe this second John Garloch should have been listed as the third or III.

On the 1810 census for Linton Hundred, Washington County, Maryland there is but one John Garlough age 26 through 44, designated by the letter D who I believe is the same as B in the earlier 1800 Census. D, or John Garloch III, now has 1 son under 10 whom I now believe was Peter Garlow, and another son 10 through 15 whom I have designated as E and believe to be John Garoch IV of the 1820 Census of German Township, Fayette County, Pennsylvania, though only named John Garloch. This Garloch would also have been Peter Garlow's older brother.

And so if I am correct we have these four John Garloch's C, A, B and D where B and D are one and the same. This makes B my 3rd great grandfather, A my 4th great grandfather, and C my 5th great grandfather. C would have been born no later than 1755 but could have been born as early as 1740.

---

[12] The Garlow name as we have observed earlier in later Federal Census Records is spelled variously as Garloch, Garlock, or Garlough.

Individual	Name	Federal Census Year	Comments
C	John Garloch	1800	Born perhaps as early as 1740 or as late as 1755
A	John Garloch Jr.	1800	Son of C & father of B
B	John Garloch Jr. (III)	1800 & 1810	Son of A
D	Same as B	1810	Father of Peter Garlow and E
E	John Garloch IV	1810	Son of D and older brother of Peter Garlow

Table I

John Garloch's by Census Year

The final question that I was unable to resolve was the whereabouts of Martin Gastmeier after he was last known to be living with his mother and step-father August Stier in 1900. Sometime between his arrival in the United States in 1882 and 1900 he is known to have married, but by 1900 had become a widower.

Figure 23 is a photo taken in July 2013 of the Arnold family during which time they were vacationing at their rented beach home in Bethany Beach Delaware. Standing left to right in the back row are the author's grandson, Ryan Mensing, the author's eldest son Charles P Arnold, III, the author and his wife Elaine, their son-in-law Michael Mensing, and wife of son Charles, Maria Arnold. Sitting on the sofa left to right are the author's son Michael Arnold, the author's eldest daughter Amy Mensing, her two daughters Katy and Rachel. Sitting on the floor are the author's youngest daughter Beth Dewey, her son Jacob, and husband Bryan Dewey.

Figure 24 is a photo of the oldest generation of Arnolds and Schusters. Standing in the back from left to right are George Schuster, Jim Agnew, and the author, Charles P Arnold, Jr. In front left to right are George's wife Marilyn, Jim's wife Judy (Nee Schuster) and the author's wife Elaine (Nee Schuster).

It is to the grandchildren mentioned above that I have dedicated this book with the hope that they or one of their children will add to the history of their family beginning with the stories of Elaine and me which began in the Spring of 1963 when the two of us met during vacation on the island of Nassau in the Bahamas.

Appendix I

Parents	Child	Grandchild	g-grandchild	gg-grandchild	ggg-grandchild
Child	Brother/ sister	Nephew/ niece	g-nephew/ g-niece	gg-nephew/ gg-niece	ggg-nephew/ ggg-niece
Grandchild	Uncle/ Aunt	First cousin	First cousin once removed	First cousin twice removed	First cousin thrice removed
g-grandchild	g-uncle/ g-aunt	First cousin once removed	Second cousin	Second cousin once removed	Second cousin twice removed
gg-grandchild	gg-uncle/ gg-aunt	First cousin twice removed	Second cousin once removed	Third cousin	Third cousin once removed
ggg-grandchild	Ggg-uncle/ ggg-aunt	First cousin thrice removed	Second cousin twice removed	Third cousin once removed	Fourth cousin

Table 2

Explanation of Cousins

5 Matthius Schuster
B:	Date unknown
	Place unknown
M:	Date unknown
	Place unknown
D:	Date unknown
	Place unknown

3 George Schuster
B:	1 Aug 1837
	Uehlfeld, Bavaria, Germany
M:	6 Oct 1867
	Place is unknown
D:	Date is unknown
	Place is unknown

6 Magdalena Schuster (Nee Bauer)
B:	Date unknown
	Place unknown
D:	Date unknown
	Place unknown

2 Margaret Schuster
B:	20 April 1862
	Warmersdorf, Bavaria, Germany
M:	
	Pennsylvania
D:	[Date]
	[Place]

7 Michael Will
B:	Date unknown
	Place unknown
M:	Date unknown
	Place unknown
D:	Date unknown
	Place unknown

4 Elizabeth Schuster (Nee Will)
B:	15 Oct 1841
	Warmersdorf, Bavaria, Germany
M:	6 Oct 1867
D:	Date is unknown
	Place is unknown

8 Mary Barbara Will (Nee Feth)
B:	Date unknown
	Place unknown
D:	Date unknown
	Place unknown

1 George Schuster
B:	22 Jan 1861
	Warmersdorf, Bavaria, Germany
M:	10 Jun 1908
	Pittsburgh, PA
D:	
	Pittsburgh, PA

Barbara Vogtmann
(Spouse)

Prepared by: Charles P Arnold, Jr., Ph.D.
[Name]
[Address]
[Phone or Email]

Date: 1 Nov 2013

Table 3

George Schuster's Family Tree

www.ingramcontent.com/pod-product-compliance
Lightning Source LLC
Chambersburg PA
CBHW030518290526
45786CB00004B/1516